NOVOCAIN

Beyond Words
Introduction to the Recovery Process

By

Virginia Beaumier

Novocain

Copyright © 2016 Virginia Beaumier. Produced by Stillwater River Publications. All rights reserved. No part of this publication may be reproduced, distributed, or transmitted in any form or by any means, including photocopying, recording, or other electronic or mechanical methods, without the prior written permission of the publisher or author, except in the case of brief quotations embodied in critical reviews and certain other noncommercial uses permitted by copyright law. Written and produced in the United States of America.

Visit our website at **www.StillwaterPress.com** for more information.

First Stillwater River Publications Edition
ISBN-10: 0-997-87783-9
ISBN-13: 978-0-997-87783-0

1 2 3 4 5 6 7 8 9 10

Publisher's Cataloging-In-Publication Data
(Prepared by The Donohue Group, Inc.)

Names: Beaumier, Virginia.
Title: Novocain : beyond words : introduction to the recovery process / by Virginia Beaumier.
Description: First Stillwater River Publications edition. | Glocester, RI, USA : Stillwater River Publications, [2016]
Identifiers: ISBN 978-0-9978778-3-0 | ISBN 0-9978778-3-9
Subjects: LCSH: Beaumier, Virginia. | Adult child sexual abuse victims--Poetry. | Child sexual abuse--Poetry. | Healing--Psychological aspects--Poetry.
Classification: LCC PS3602.E29 B43 2016 | DDC 811.6--dc23

Written by Viriginia Beaumier
Cover & Interior Design by Dawn M. Porter

Published by Stillwater River Publications, Glocester, RI, USA.

The views and opinions expressed in this book are solely those of the author and do not necessarily reflect the views and opinions of the publisher.

Dedication

As children we are innocent and sometimes without realization our siblings comfort and support us.

To my brother Robert and especially my six children Bert, Bruce, Michael, Elizabeth, Benjamin and Annie.

And a very special thank you to my granddaughter Lindsey who has been most helpful in putting my pages together.

"Forgiveness is the fragrance the violet sheds on the heel that has crushed it."

-- *Mark Twain*

BELIEVE

I couldn't tell
Scared as hell
Who would believe a kid?

And if I did
Who would listen
Who would believe a kid?

When the time is right
And you will know
Who would believe that kid?
Everyone
Everyone
I know because I did

FORGIVE

To forgive is sublime
And you will in due time
Or how will you take
That next step

To move forward in peace
While destroying the beast
And all of the tears
That you wept

INNOCENT

That person inside you needs you
Reach out and call her by name

She was just a child
Without a voice
Waiting for you and you came
To speak to her
To rescue her
And love her with all that you are

You're the only one who can show her
The way to be rid of that scar

FAITH AND HOPE

In healing
You can slowly take back
All of the time that you've lost
If you have but just a little

Each day will bring you closer
To a world awaiting you
If you have but just a little

It's faith you know
And hope to grow
If you have but just a little

CROCODILE

Crocodile
Pedophile
Creeping all around

Waiting for that moment
Where innocence is found

GOD'S GRACE

Welcome and rest easy
You've made it to that place

I know that run and it's over
You're no longer in that race

You feel a sense of freedom
A smile is replaced

All this and more
Is on its way
I'm thankful for God's grace

UNKNOWN

I've never even seen your face
But we share a bond
A common place
And I know you

Your sorrow is transparent
To me who knows your pain
With time and understanding
You will have much more to gain

MONSTERS

The Mayas
The Oprahs
Even you and I

The professors
And the students
And there is no reason why

You're a monster on the loose
And you know who you are
You'll never get away with this

We've worked too hard
We've come too far

YOUR PLACE IN THIS WORLD

The music you hear is crescendo
And the colors you see have stirred

A vocal and vibrant new you
You have what it takes to be heard

CONCRETE ANGEL

You're the concrete angel
We hear about in song
You're quiet and shy
And you think
You don't belong

I remember a time
When I felt as you do
Discouraged and saddened
By what I knew

Beneath all that sadness
A secret storm
A broken heart
With dreams unknown

A POWERFUL YOU

I'M SORRY

A small I'm sorry
Is all it takes

To validate innocence
Taken by snakes

HEART AND SOUL

Why have tears soak up your face
Why be faceless in a place
That needs the heart and soul of you

Why have darkness
You are light

Guide your spirit
Show your face
Reap and embrace this worldly place
That needs the heart and soul of you

PATIENCE

Give yourself the time
Patience is the pause
It refreshes and replaces
For you and your cause

It's forgiving and quiet
And constant and calm
Never in vain
And all without qualm

THE TAPE MEASURE

There is no tape to measure pain
Those suffering years were not in vain
And there's not enough rain
To wash it away
But that sun will shine
On your healing day

There is no cure yet healing begins
The numbness starts to fade
And in return
Abundance strength
For the price that you have paid

3 6 5

There will be days of sadness
Days of heartache and contempt
Days of feeling down and lonely
Days of thought with no exempt

Those are days when you may feel
You've done all that you can
And for today — it may just be
The timing in God's plan

COURAGE

Getting in touch with feelings inside
Will come as a ripple and wave
And sometimes bring a light of hope
Like a storm
Then a leap for the brave

It's courage you know you already have
You knew it all along
Finally it's out in the open
Those feelings are brand new
And strong

NAMES

Scandal Scandal
That's your handle

Shame Shame
You're to blame

Traitor Traitor
Perpetrator

You've earned this name
In your "Hall of Fame"

AGAPE

Let the truth be wide open
It's a God sized event
To expose and reveal
And with every intent

Let your silence be broken
From a paralyzed heart
With no words left unspoken
Flowing right from the start

Stay hungry for the healing
Your release point is quite near
When all is said and all is done
It all becomes quite clear

DEMONS

A betrayal of innocence
A twisted mind
The demons of your past

That dark side of existence
Was never meant to last

Because your world of darkness
Will one day change to light
You've made a choice
You have a voice
Your courage made it right

KELOID

The present moment is tolerable
And your healing is at hand
I'm speaking from a keloid heart
That bears the same
And I understand

Your innocence was taken
When your life had just begun
A life so filled with promise
So what else could you have done

Your impenetrable disguise
Has suddenly burst
You rely on the desire
That you come first

DREAMS

There was a time I couldn't dream
Back then – I didn't know why
It was always just a nightmare
Not a dream and I would cry

Being chased by a monster
Fed my childish mind with fear
But now my dreams are vivid
My mind is free and clear

One day you will awaken and find
That truth will set you free
And all your dreams just may come
True
And you will dream like me

IF I COULD

Your eyes are fixed
Your mind is mixed
And I would change that
If I could

Your heart is torn
Your thoughts are worn
And I would change that
If I could

Your silence is loud
And I hear you
I know you'd speak up
If you could

And one day you will
And you won't be still
When you tell the world
As you should

IN THE DARK

I was a child robbed in the dark
Finally I know this
I have sliced my numbness open
With the blades of my own eyes

From years of watching
I have grown the pupils of a cat
And now
I am able to see in that dark

ABOUT THE AUTHOR

Virginia Beaumier is the Christian mother of six wonderful children, a nurse, and an incest survivor.

Made in the USA
Middletown, DE
10 October 2023